FUNNY BUNNY JOKES

by Stephanie Calmenson
illustrated by Don Orehek

SCHOLASTIC INC.
New York Toronto London Auckland Sydney

To Joanna, Phil, and Rachel

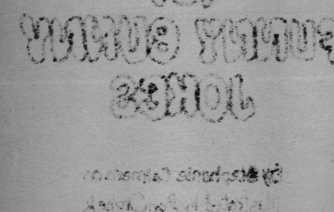

ISBN 0-590-43165-X

12 11 10   5/9

Printed in the U.S.A.   01

First Scholastic printing, March 1990

RABBIT RIB-TICKLERS

What happened when five hundred hares got loose on Main Street?

The police had to comb the area.

What did the magician say when he made his rabbit disappear?

Hare today, gone tomorrow.

Where do rabbits go after their wedding?

On their bunnymoon.

Why did the bald man put a rabbit on his head?

He needed the hare.

Where do you find rabbits?

Wherever you leave them!

Down-on-His-Luck Rabbit: I got kicked out of my cage for not paying the rent. My wife walked out and took our twenty-nine bunnies with her. I'm all out of carrots. What should I do?

Helpful Friend: Don't worry; be hoppy!

What is a twip?

A twip is what a wabbit takes when he wides a twain.

When is an elephant like a cute little bunny rabbit?

When he's wearing his cute little bunny-rabbit suit.

What's the difference between a hare and a mare?

One letter.

What is the difference between a rabbit and a flea?

A rabbit can have fleas, but a flea can't have rabbits.

FUNNY BUNNY HINK PINKS

What do you call a chocolate Easter bunny that was out in the sun too long?

A runny bunny.

Why do rabbits go to the beauty parlor?

For hare care.

What do you call the everyday routines of rabbits?

Rabbit's habits.

What do you call a rabbit with no clothes on?

A bare hare.

What do you call an unusual rabbit?

A rare hare.

What do you call it when one rabbit challenges another rabbit to hop across a forty-yard canyon?

A *hare dare.*

CARROT CAPERS

How do you know carrots are good for your eyes?

Did you ever see a rabbit wearing glasses?

What did the rabbit bride get on her wedding day?

A forty-carrot wedding ring.

What is furry, has two thousand eyes, and eats carrots?

One thousand rabbits.

What's the best way to catch a rabbit?

Hide behind a bush and make a noise like a carrot.

WHAT DO YOU GET?

What do you get when you cross a
bumble bee with a rabbit?

A honey bunny.

What do you get when you cross a rabbit with a comedian?

A funny bunny.

What do you get when you cross a frog and a rabbit?

A rabbit that says, "Ribbit."

What do you get when you cross a
rabbit with a millionaire?

A bunny with money.

What do you get when you cross a
rabbit with strawberry soda?

A berry bubbly bunny.

JACK RABBIT JOKES

Jack Rabbit: Do you feel like a glass of carrot juice?

Betty Badger: Why? Do I look like one?

Jack Rabbit: What do you call a rabbit who is real cool?
Bill Bear: A hip hopper.

Jack Rabbit: Can you say "Richard and Robert had a rabbit" without using the "r" sound?

Ollie Owl: I don't think so. Can you?

Jack Rabbit: Sure. Dick and Bob had a bunny.

Jack Rabbit: I'm sure glad I'm not a bird. I could get hurt!

Moe Mouse: Why is that?

Jack Rabbit: I can't fly.

WHAT'S THE QUESTION?

Answer: *A hopsicle.*
Question: What is a rabbit's
favorite dessert?

Answer: *Bellhop.*
Question: What job do rabbits at hotels have?

Answer: *Hop rods.*
Question: What kind of cars do rabbits drive?

RABBIT FAVORITES

Favorite movie:
Rabbits of the Lost Ark.

Favorite book:
Hop on Pop.

Favorite song:
"Hoppy Birthday to You."

Favorite musical:
Hare.

Favorite TV show:
Hoppy Days.

Favorite dance:
The bunny hop.

WHAT'S UP, DOC?

Rabbit: Doctor, I have carrots growing out of my ears.
Doctor: Yes, I see. How did that happen?
Rabbit: I don't know. I planted lettuce.

Rabbit: Doctor, I'm feeling funny today. What should I do?
Doctor: Go on television.

Nurse: How is the rabbit who swallowed the quarter?

Doctor: No change yet.

Nurse: What do you call an operation on a rabbit?

Doctor: A hare-cut.

First Rabbit: Did you hear about the doctor who cut off the rabbit's left side by mistake?

Second Rabbit: No, I didn't. How's the rabbit?

First Rabbit: He's all right now.

Rabbit: My friend is nuts. He thinks he's Bugs Bunny. But I'm positive he isn't.

Doctor: How do you know he isn't?

Rabbit: Because I am.

Rabbit: Doctor, I have a terrible earache.

Doctor: Have you ever had an earache before?

Rabbit: Yes, twice last year.

Doctor: Well, you've got one again.

Rabbit: Are you sure this bottle of special carrot juice will cure me?

Doctor: Absolutely. No rabbit ever came back for another.

Rabbit: Doctor, when I get well
   will I be able to play the piano?
Doctor: Of course.
Rabbit: That's great. I was never
   able to play it before.

RED, WHITE, AND BLUE BUNNIES

What is white, with long ears, whiskers, and sixteen wheels?

Two white rabbits on roller skates.

What do you do with a blue rabbit?

Cheer him up.

Why are rabbits never gold?

How would you tell them apart from goldfish?

How is a rabbit like a plum?

They're both purple, except for the rabbit.

WORLD-FAMOUS
RABBITS

Which rabbit is a famous comedian?

Bob Hop.

Which rabbit stole from the rich to give to the poor?

Rabbit Hood.

Which rabbits were famous bank robbers?

Bunny and Clyde.

Which rabbit was a famous female aviator?

Amelia Harehart.

Which rabbit was in Western
movies?

Hopalong Cassidy.

JOKES FOR THE WELL-DRESSED RABBIT

Why did the rabbit wear red suspenders?

To keep his pants up.

Selma Rabbit: Do you think that's Sophie's natural color?
Sam Rabbit: Only her hare dresser knows for sure.

What should a rabbit use to keep his fur neat?

A *harebrush*.

When do rabbits wear green overalls?

When their blue ones are in the laundry.

What do you know when you see
three rabbits walking down the
street wearing tuxedos and top
hats?

You know you need a psychiatrist!

BABY! BABY!

What do rabbits have that no other
animals have?

Baby rabbits.

When do rabbits have buck teeth?

When their parents won't get them braces.

What is a rabbit after it is five days old?

Six days old.

What game do bunnies like best?

Hopscotch.

Baby Rabbit: Mommy, where did I come from?

Mother Rabbit: I'll tell you when you're older.

Baby Rabbit: Oh, Mommy, please, tell me now.

Mother Rabbit: If you must know, you were pulled from a magician's hat.

DINING OUT

Rabbit Diner: Waiter, what is this hare doing in my salad?

Waiter: I believe he's eating your lettuce.

Rick and Rita Rabbit were out on their first date at a French restaurant. Rick was showing off.

"I'm studying French this year and I'm getting really good at it," said Rick.

"That's wonderful," said Rita.

Just then the waiter came over. "Say something in French," whispered Rita to Rick.

So Rick said, "Something in French."

A rabbit and a duck went to a restaurant for dinner. Who paid?

The duck because he had the bill.

Why did the rabbit run out of the fast-food restaurant?

He thought he heard someone order a quarter pounder on a toasted bunny.

GO, BUNNIES, GO!

What's the fastest way to send a rabbit?

Haremail.

How far can a rabbit run into the woods?

Halfway. After that she's running out of the woods.

Why couldn't the rabbit fly home for Easter?

He didn't have the hare fare.

RIDICULOUS RABBITS

A woman found a rabbit inside her refrigerator. "What are you doing in there?" she asked.

"This is a Westinghouse, isn't it?" said the rabbit.

"Yes, it is," said the woman.

"Well, I'm westing," the rabbit said.

Which rabbits have the smallest feet?

The smallest rabbits.

Did you hear about the rabbit who got a job in a watch factory?

All he did was stand around making faces.

TONGUE-TWISTER TRIO

Roger Rabbit's red Rolls Royce
rolled right.

Harry Hare held Hatty Hare's hat.

Brenda's bunnies bake buttered
bread.

HOW DO YOU. . . ?

How do you make a rabbit stew?

Keep it waiting.

How do you make a rabbit fast?

Don't feed it.

How do you know when there's a
rabbit in your bed?

*You can smell the carrots on his
breath.*

How do you shake hands with a
hundred-pound bunny?

Very carefully.

How do you make a rabbit float?

Put soda, syrup, and milk into a glass. Add one rabbit.

WHY? WHY? WHY?

Why don't rabbits finish college?

Because they don't finish high school.

Why was the rabbit's nose shiny?

She was wearing her powder puff on the wrong end.

Why can't a rabbit's nose be twelve inches long?

Because then it would be a foot.

Why are rabbits like calculators?

They both multiply a lot.

BUNNIES IN SCHOOL

Teacher: If you had sixteen jelly beans and Jack asked you for ten of them, how many jelly beans would you have left?

Jill: Sixteen.

Timmy Rabbit: Mom, I got a hundred in school today!

Mother Rabbit: That's great! What did you get a hundred in?

Timmy Rabbit: In two things — fifty in math and fifty in spelling.

Teacher: How did you find the test questions?

Smart-Aleck Bunny: Easy. It was finding the answers that was hard.

Three rabbits went to school under the same umbrella. Why didn't they get wet?

It wasn't raining.

FUNNY BUNNY KNOCK-KNOCKS

Knock-knock.
Who's there?
Hoppy.
Hoppy who?
Hoppy to see you.

Knock-knock.
Who's there?
Ron.
Ron who?
Ron! Ron! The hunters are coming.

Knock-knock.

Who's there?

Ken.

Ken who?

Ken I give you some jelly beans?

Knock-knock.

Who's there?

Tommy.

Tommy who?

Tommy ache 'cause I ate all the jelly beans.

Knock-knock.
Who's there?
Madge.
Madge who?
Madge-ician pulled a rabbit from
his hat.

Knock-knock.
Who's there?
Ida.
Ida who?
Ida know any more bunny knock-
    knocks.

CALLING ALL RABBITS!

What do you call an affectionate rabbit?

A *tender, loving hare.*

How many chocolate bunnies can you put into an empty Easter basket?

One. After that the basket won't be empty.

Why did the rabbit cross the road?

Because the chicken had his Easter eggs.

What do you call an easy-going
rabbit?

Hoppy-go-lucky.

What do you call a rabbit with
fleas?

Bugs Bunny.

EASTER BUNNY FUNNIES

Molly Mole: What's the difference between the Easter rabbit and a mattababy?

Barney Beaver: What's a mattababy?

Molly Mole: Nothing. What's the matter with you?

Where do Easter bunnies dance?

At the basketball.

HARE'S SOME MORE!

When does a rabbit go exactly as fast as a train?

When it's on the train.

A woman was riding a horse through the woods when she passed a rabbit.

"Good morning," said the rabbit.

The woman rode a little way, then said, "I didn't know rabbits could talk."

"Neither did I," said her horse.

A bumble bee was chasing a rabbit.
Finally the bee turned around and
flew away. Why?

The rabbit had two b's already.

Why did the rabbit put wheels on her rocking chair?

She wanted to rock and roll.

Why did the dirty rabbit cross the road twice?

He was a dirty double-crosser.

Which side of a rabbit has the most fur?

The outside.

Johnny's rabbit was playing games on the computer when Johnny's father walked in.

"That rabbit is amazing!" said Johnny's father.

"Not really," said Johnny. "He's already lost three games."

What book did the rabbit take on vacation?

One with a hoppy ending.